EVERYTHING INDICATES

First published in 2023 by Blue Diode Press.
30 Lochend Road
Leith
Edinburgh EH6 8BS
www.bluediode.co.uk

ISBN: 978-1-915108-15-9.

Thanks to the Czech Republic Ministry of Culture for a grant towards the production of this book.

**MINISTRY OF CULTURE
CZECH REPUBLIC**

Typesetting: Rob A. Mackenzie and Amy Curtis.
text in Dante MT Pro.

Cover art and design: Internoia.
http://www.internoia.com

Diode logo design: Sam and Ian Alexander.

Printed and bound by Imprint Digital, Exeter, UK.
https://digital.imprint.co.uk

EVERYTHING INDICATES
Selected Poems

Petr Hruška
translated by Jonathan Bolton

BLUE DIODE PRESS
EDINBURGH

Contents

The Door

The door always used to swing shut, by itself, for years and years, with measured haste.

Now it stands utterly still.

Next to it, a woman guiltily picks up a large undershirt that fell from the line overnight. A man watches the woman with the shirt. Probably the wind. During the night.

Both would like to know when, when exactly it happened. Both would like to be in that moment.

Last Century

We used to drink somewhere in the marketplace. Or at the bus stop, in winter coats, next to pieces of fiberboard. We were in a hurry, we had our whole shared life ahead of us. We wanted to catch it, that flickering among the cardboard and the sellers, that drinking with tender, icy hands.

Early Spring

They had already sat down on the bed. Then the man remembered the back door was still open. He groped along the hallway, past the dark holes of workshops and spaces. Past the dark holes of sleeves on the communal coat stand. The house was wide open, pulled inside out.

His hand on the latch, he saw the last stretch of snow by the hazel bushes under the roof. It lay there white and large, like an animal with its head raised, like a bared shoulder. Like, when all is said and done, several things in life. It lay there white and incongruous, by the backyard door.

He groped his way back, slowly and quietly, in case his wife was already asleep.

Night

True darkness is in a child's bedroom. Deep black. Elsewhere there's just a meager, watery twilight, in which everything, in the end, acquires a humiliating distinctness.

Place

Maybe poplars or elms. It's as if the wind meant to give a sermon. Your dress with the ships is billowing. I know where it usually hangs in the closet. Its yellow colour, fading out in the mist by the road.

We go back to the car. We stopped for some insignificant reason, now dispatched. We'll never find this here again, nor these trees that have been set swaying, elms, probably.

Nothing

She shook him like an autumn branch: *Somebody's here.* But when he got up and switched on the light in the next room, all that appeared was the reliability of things, just the radio and the meat they had put out to thaw, waiting for morning. Just the tall mullein flowers standing by the wall outside, like men next to a pub on a clear night.

Everything Indicates

They are sitting there, flecked by the morning sun. Everything indicates that the woman will take away the mugs and then stay in the kitchen.

But suddenly she begins to talk about a blizzard in Switzerland. About gusts of wind shaking her young body so hard that she turned around, thinking it was a man's hand. Amidst the madly whirling snow.

They sit in the sun, and he can't understand: how is it possible he didn't know about the blizzard in Switzerland until today.

Two

Two days of rain. Children on the floor. Scant trees.

The furniture confesses to the boards. Reaching for something in reserve, my wife stretches way back, behind the boxes of receipts and birthday candles. A bit of her stomach appears, forgivably, like a slip of the tongue in a long eulogy.

-

★★★

An overturned bucket of white, meant for painting the church's ceiling. The paint spilled on the floor has hardened into its own object, a wild white rag.

I'm not looking for God here. I'm looking for the painter with white fingers, for that clumsy human movement.

Inversion

A day without a sky. The city is muffled in fog so thick a drunkard could lean against it, wracked by an evil wind.

The lights are on in the Asian bistro even though it is noon. In the kitchen next door, between the tall refrigerators, some people are laughing silently at a joke in Vietnamese.

Tomorrow

Moths, pale as clenched fingers, sleep among the pipes overhead. Yesterday someone must have been looking into the darkness above the viaduct, for a long, long time, the open, illuminated apartment behind them.

The Silent One

That's him.
It happens.
Selective mutism,
as learned people call it,
the sudden loss of speech.
From one day to the next,
a person presses his hands to his body,
his mouth turns into a line,
he no longer gives out a word,
a sob,
or even a sigh.
Instead of laughter, and then only rarely,
there is a mute grin,
crying without tears.
He doesn't even talk in his sleep.
In the midst of others, he stands
all lengthwise,
like a fright or a threat.
Cause unknown.
The doctors say not to pressure him,
and so the others
mostly just turn up the volume,
waving their hands,
speaking more vehemently now, and more often,
speaking for him as well.

Barking

The mother watches
as her son imitates a retriever.
He is twenty-seven,
she is forty-five,
both of them up to their necks in the world.
They've tried everything,
mainly classified ads and doctors.
Apparently both are believers.
Both come regularly to this all-night bar.
They are as real as the hook
of beauty.
The son leaning against the table,
the mother motionless, listening
how far the sound travels here,
the barking of the retriever.

Scratch

How can you sing so clearly
so late at night?
Among the cartridge cases, fired in a rage,
of bottles on the ground.
Among the angry dogs on their long legs
and the scraps of plastic
that are nearly as fast.
Among the black vipers
of thrown-away tyres.

Decent people sleep through destruction.
But you sing
as straightforwardly as
a scratch reveals hematite.
In a moment
late will spill over into early
and then there will be nothing to hear
in the gathering screech
of awakening.

My Boy

My boy!
You saw me
carrying a full bottle.
You looked attentively
at my fingers.
You listened
to those idiots cutting down walnut trees in the street,
one after another,
to give the city a new look.
Yesterday someone on the internet offered you
another life.
You crumpled and smoothed
your cap
when your mother asked me
if I knew what love means.

You have her eyes and my fingers.
You're ready,
my boy.

Wait a moment.
The smoke from the morning cafeteria
is rising into a confused strip of sunlight
and changing
into orange smoke.

———

By the river today
you were shouting something at me
over the turbid rushing waters
and I didn't understand.
It sounded like

To no travail!
To no fucking travail!

The river was terribly long.
You were shouting at me,
my boy,
waving a half-rotten branch,
and your eyes were wide open.
Like a line of credit.

———

Out on the balcony, I prepared
a tomato salad
in this undermined city.
Will you remember it?
The unruly pieces of red
in the glass bowls
on the edge of the concrete windowsill
in August.
In short, a celebration.

I was lying to you the whole time,
my boy,
when I said that I didn't keep company with futility.
That I went to bed right after you
and wasn't out alone on my desperate, doubtful wanderings,
where a bare lightbulb hung from the ceiling like a testicle.
I was lying when I said
that the splatter marks on the walls
made good maps,
that I had read our contract with the world
and it was written in comprehensible lettering,
similar to your mother's handwriting.
I was lying.
Only the tomatoes on the concrete
are the truth.

A Real Tuna

for Jan Balabán

Oh, to get a real tuna
so the inextinguishable fish-silver
shakes us up
when it's slapped down on the pages
of a dead newspaper meant for fish
A real tuna
enough to make us feel
once again
a good long chill in our wrists
above the heavy silver of the world
carry it past
the steep backs
of the banking houses
and then unwrap the newspaper at home
the pre-election faces stained with fish-oil
look out with an even more devious leer
a great body in the shallows of the newspaper
the shallows of the table
A real tuna
that sends ripples through
the laundered ruffles of domestic silence
until suddenly, damn it, we remember
everything we
wanted here

The Garden

the garden in disrepair
the autumn rain at the slant
of the twine that supported the bean vines
the autumn rain at the slant
of the handwriting in a message
saying when you will come

While We're in the Kitchen

We would drive into the darkness
the yellow branches of wild-growing maples
would reach greedily
toward the car
Somewhere off to the side
there would be a chapel covered in scrawls
but there wouldn't have to be
nor a discarded piece of rain-battered tin
there wouldn't have to be anything there
We would get out
stand next to each other
helplessly, firmly
in our sweaters and in the headlights
beautiful steam rising from our mouths
Only then
would I head down
to ask for directions

A Room for the Night

the big trucks roared like ravenous
beasts of the night
you called out the price to me
a room for two people
the guy from the gas station
angular with lack of sleep
led us up a steep staircase
Berlin Krakow Trieste all of it
was in the past now
I had never seen
such a narrow room
when we wanted to turn around
we had to embrace

In the Centre

The Cultural Centre at the train station
an empty room with vases
and a shelf of books
pointlessly thick books
In a while we'll be gone
the distant hum
the rushing sky
Come we'll open this one together
Seventeenth-Century Flemish Painting
and we'll look for a while
at the glimmering carafes
the pewter of the candlestick
the grapes and the knife

Looking Through

As if it were an old Dutch painting
he sees, through an open door,
another open door
and only then
part of a woman's figure
standing on cold tiles,
bent, persisting, over
a motionless rivulet
of household water

Before Bathing

you took off your clothes
with forty-year-old hands
and you turned
to the drawers
where for such a terribly long time
we've kept creams razors and tools
I turned my eyes away
from this beauty
and all I remember
is the white spine
of a book about Giotto

Theft

Our things from the stolen satchel
must have been thrown, in disappointment,
in a pile at some quiet spot by the river:
the checked shirt,
the envelopes,
the red hairband.

They must be lying somewhere in the snow,
forever, unused.
Once in a while the envelopes stir.
The blue colour weighs down the shirt.
When was the last time
we were so together?

Puffins

in those days when
the damp concrete was constantly filthy
with blossoms fallen from the trees
we met a few times
at an unusual hour
in some bistro or bar
not far from the apartment we shared
each of us would arrive
from a different direction
we would sit across from each other
observing our ever more visible faces
lit up by the day
we listened to our words
where do they come from
flying back and forth
in small flocks
like puffins from their inaccessible cliffs
in the northern seas
we arranged more
and more meetings
in those days that were filthy
with blossoms fallen from the trees

Orange Milk-Caps

There was nothing there
just a scrawl of leafless bushes
at the edge of the forest
and the littered scraps of siskins
and the ominous white light of an afternoon
from after the completion of the world
Then she found
the first milk-cap
an orange stain in the grass's old age
and then he too found
another one
then they kept finding them
beneath the scrawls of the bushes
the stains leapt out
and spread, itching, in all directions
wherever they turned their gaze
they couldn't gather them all
In this completed world
they stood
scorched by the orange abundance
of milk-caps in the fall

Evening Shop

Food in a sour outpouring of light.
It was already like this under the communists.
Just two types of everything,
the dialectic of beans, wine, chocolate,
except for vodka.
The bottles and cans are pressed together
like a wall
over which tomorrow slowly crawls.
And there was always
a woman in the storeroom in back.
She was arranging or carrying something,
something simple and important
was stirring back there,
as if she were balancing out
the depths of the night,
while a person in line
watched the Baltic sardines
vanish irreversibly into someone else's hands.

Marymount in Ostrava

a window open at night
drinking from a paper bag
a gathering next to the gas station
Mars is very close
for these people arriving from the darkness,
around forty years old or older
the presence of cryptoendolithic organisms
beneath the rocks there
cannot be ruled out
by the gas station it's someone's birthday
drinking from a paper bag
they take turns raising their heads
it cannot be ruled out
that the dark spots on some rocks
indicate the presence of life

Fire

A frightful knife
that could kill a bear.
The soup with the rust of his forty years.
Damp matches in the sleeves of his workshirt.
The impoverished brushwood from leafy trees.

Everything seems dramatic
and yet it's just a few hundred metres
from the rows of garages.
A person –
from a distance he looks like a figure in a cave painting –
stands here, curses,
keeps bending over and straightening up.

Staring vacantly,
the clump of bushes forgot itself for a moment,
but now it's also wandering off through the afternoon.
Nothing has been decided.
Like a delicate weed
a pale fire grows here,
finally ignited
in the middle of the work week
a few hundred metres beyond the garages.

Face

The Ukrainian woman slept curled up
like someone
who knows how to conserve space, warmth,
maybe even a dream.
Now she is sitting up again.
The spot on her face
looks like old age,
a prickling rash she's had since childhood,
a recent outbreak of fever,
concealed lamentation.
Or just the imprint from the seat
of the international express
hurtling
through an endless plain
and its tall, silent grass.

After the Disaster

Put your things here for now.

Someone has made space on a shelf,
in a drawer or closet.
And after the disaster someone
is laying out their personal things here,
their wretched and proud things.

It doesn't matter what happened.
It doesn't matter what orphanage we're in.
Everything retreats before the terrible beauty
of this *for now,*
in which someone is straightening what remains.

Mock Orange

you wipe off the tabletop in vain
that's not a spill
from inside the household
it's the malevolent bush
of mock orange in spring
casting its shadow from the garden

The Undergrowth in Finland

I, who am not here,
have been yearning this whole time to see
a polar fox – in vain
But not you
you simply see one
as it runs out
of some meaningless Finnish undergrowth
stops
and raises its white head to you
this is how you see everything
whenever you arrive somewhere
you can't help it
soon you will be full
of fox heads

Worn-Away Bas-Relief

There are no more lions here.
Only their paws, crushing a bull,
who is dying in the classical manner,
from the depths.

God forbid
I should ever go astray
in those regions where only
the pawless lions roam.

Daughter

I hope a car runs me over
while I'm out
getting the bread!
you shouted
into the household

For the whole time
you were gone
life stood still inside me
austere
like a Doric column

Sit down at the table now
take the butter
as hard and white as a wall
and get ready –

we'll be eating for a long time

Sleet and Snow

He got up in the early morning
to walk his daughter to the train station
it was snowing unpleasantly
and as her orange hat
was receding into the distance
he suddenly realized
that it was almost too early
that nothing was open yet
not even the newsstand
it was too early
for news from the world
for waking up the drunks in the entryway
for proper faith proper
despair
for conversation
because at this snow-filled hour
there might not even be speech
only the thin trunks of the streetlamps
the unemployment of the city
and a quiet remainder of sleep with his wife
at this hour
after seeing off his daughter

Titan

On Saturn's moon Titan
there is a wild methane sea
It seems there are
frozen cliffs, orange in colour,
emerging from it

You came to tell me this
with a fixed stare
your arms hanging by your sides
The cupboards
propping up the walls

The pipe stupidly yellow
how many years

And now
the sudden unexpected closeness of those
who know
about Titan's sea

Shoe

Take off the shoe.
It's the last children's size.
The instructions on the glue bottle
are printed in tauntingly small type –
you'll have to read them.
We lean
over the filthy wet shoe.
We'll roughen the surface of the rubber
and let the chemical process go to work inside the crack.
Keep in mind
that our bodies, too, are made of oxygen and carbon
from ancient stars.
Distant, solitary stars.
You talk about Mom.
So put your finger on the loop,
we'll use the shoelaces to pull the glued-on sole tight.
The night zooming by,
the crazily bound shoe.
The last children's size.

***

And I saw
how scrawny it was,
the letter to the sanatorium,
although it contained all the reasons
it made sense to come back
here,
to the world of reasons.

Yesterday, when the growing boy
stretched out his arm,
they pulled on a leather glove with a bird of prey,
striped and silent.
Both of them suddenly
felt
a living weight.

Call Jaroslav

and, first, prepare
two or three reasons
why he shouldn't start
drinking again
see if you can get him
to sell that house,
to go down to the garden
and feed the cats,
in the worst case tell him again
what the wind is just now doing
with the bouquets of lilac
by the mailboxes out front
and then make a note in your datebook:
call Jaroslav

Also

No bright light shining through,
just a yellowish illumination,
like when cucumbers bloom
on your windowsill.
Like the light cast by tea for someone
struggling with alcohol.

And yet it's enough
to recognize
that there is also love here.
The courage, that is,
to exchange God
for a prayer.

A Walker in the Night

I recognize her by her gait,
by the bags she carries.
She reaches the end of the night street
and laughs
as if she were standing above an abyss.
As if she knew
that no path leads any further
and she herself
will now have to create
the entire continuation
of this crazy city,
which looks, in the mornings, so convincing.

The Cat

Animals have a much better grasp
of the fundamentals of geometry.
The black cat soon locates
the pivot of a situation,
the centre of a place,
the golden mean of the afternoon, and settles down there.

In the middle of the night it sits up,
sharpens its silhouette,
and ascertains
that it doesn't belong anywhere.

The Great Hall

They've already started construction.
It will be big,
many say the biggest.
Made of those thin quickly-growing walls,
where grass will rustle delicately
in the summer.
Its greyness will stretch all the way to the mountains.
Anything at all will fit inside,
for a long time to come.
Anything at all, if necessary,
and all at the same time.
It will encompass as much as possible.
A shout won't even reach
the other end,
but will grow faint along the way.
So it will finally be here,
a really big
multi-purpose hall,
as befits our age.
They've already started construction.

Pillar

Reinforced concrete is reinforced concrete.
The pale pillar aims callously
upwards,
breaking through lowness.
At its base there is an undergrowth
of wildly blooming graffiti,
piss stains,
the nervousness of leaves.
But the pillar rises higher,
disappears from sight,
amidst murky scraps of fog.
The trunk of reinforced concrete
as befits our age
is larger than the embrace of five men.
There must be something up there.
There has to be,
when a pillar like this
is standing here.

The World for a Moment

It happens on the dark
stairway down.
He is hurriedly pulling off his gloves
and turning to her.
Her mouth is slightly open,
her arm half-raised.
The petrified dizziness of the iron staircase
slowly awakens.
His back brushes against a switch,
in the spotlight's flash appear columns and corbels,
joists, girders, and screws,
intersecting supports.
All the interlocking vault of the gigantic hall
created suddenly above them
in a moment of light.

The Newspaper in Bucharest

The Romanian newspaper full of unclear news reports
about the ubiquitous tremors
will have to do.
It has been pouring for days.
When he arrives at the Hotel Michelangelo
his shoes are soaked through
and in his room he stuffs them with
the Romanian newspaper
full of unclear news reports and horoscopes.
In the morning he gazes at the crumpled paper.

Today he will leave –
because she is not here.
They must have missed each other.

He's already standing outside.
On the floor in the Hotel Michelangelo
remains the absurdity
of an entire Carpathian mountain range
made of newspaper.

You'll See

Turn around
to where you slept last night
and you'll see it's absolutely temporary
the fragile dead blanket
the crumpled sphere of action
the water in the ominously old cup
you'll see how you tried
to exist
and wait it out
how at one point a dream
tossed you around
how a wasteland was always spreading off
in all directions
from where you lay
how you dug your way out
and stood up once more
against the terrible speed of light

Entrance

How rudely the rainy day's meaning
crashed into us!
By mistake we left
through the back entrance
of the indifferent westward-facing hotel,
stepping out among the motorbikes and fisherman's buckets
The cold idleness of the equipment
feathers trembling on the ground
Out front we owed
for a night's lodging
our luggage was lying out front
our documents waiting
Here the white open space
wordlessly chopped off heads
Most conspicuous was a tree
brawling to a stand-off with the wind

A Market in Frankfurt

A fit of hopelessness convulsed her in the shopping
centre.
She had to lean all her weight against a shelf
and bury her hands in the spaghetti,
which began to spill out, fan-like, in all directions.
She kept on
without it making any sense.
Her body stopped denying
its total abandonment.
Her necklace hung taut in a beautiful emptiness.
The years protruded
like ribs
in the store's perfect illumination,
which cast no shadows.
An assistant came to add more lobsters.
She stood there,
tall and unconquerable,
beneath her a wild star
of scattered spaghetti.

The Bank in Amsterdam

I'm sorry,
the woman said to the whole bank.
It carried through the discreet, glassed-in hush,
I'm sorry,
she said sympathetically,
in the air-conditioned, evenly distributed coolness
that turned the pale skin
of her bare arms and legs
into marble,
I'm sorry.
It sounded from a distance.
It sounded from childhood,
from the places where life has been gathered.
The bank floated through the morning,
serious and slow,
like an aircraft carrier.
I'm sorry,
the woman said into those empty
triumphant spaces,
as if she knew more,
much more.
A shared story was trembling there,
represented by that woman
repeating one last time
I'm sorry.

The Flower Shop in Livorno

You're standing in front of a flower shop in Livorno
and you realize –
it is precisely unimportant

The day slopes down heavily toward the docks
lays siege to the fortress
solemnly ascends the steps of city hall
the steps of the bell tower

You step inside
the shadows of leaves slide over your body
you hear your own breathing
you think of those few people
whose breathing
you have heard

You step inside
into your own precise unimportance

The Two of Us Again

We pushed through the afternoon's
wet leaves.
The shit-covered clearing bathed in light.
There should have been more here,
after so many years.
There should have been a sign,
or an outline,
or a direction.
No.
The two of us,
wet from the afternoon leaves.

On Deck in Normandy

I arrived at the miserable railing
where you were standing.
Both of us grasped
the metal crossbar
like a surprising, cold gift.

Beneath us, cars emerged from the ship.
Long trucks
loaded to the top
with newly minted automobiles.
They didn't stop in the port but continued on,
toward the victory arches
of the highway entrance ramps.

The evening sky crashed above us.
We stood there
and kept our eyes on those vehicles carrying vehicles,
on those new, utterly empty cars
racing motionless down the highway.

I Am Growing Old

for James Wright

Her hands poke out of her shirt like laughter.
A bird's cry
falls into a corner of the garden.
There is my mother,
sitting on a chair,
her back to me.

Cross Out

I wanted to finish.
I wanted to have it all done,
have no debts,
conclude things properly.
To go through everything again,
find the remaining mistakes,
the blank and fragmentary places,
the injustices.
I wanted to fix everything somehow,
fill it out, explain.
The cat breathed the night in, through a crevice in the window.
I wanted to get to the end
so it could all turn out somehow,
and so I would know how.
Until I saw my wife,
sleeping,
exhausted from quarrels, from hoping,
one arm placed on her chest
like a white line.

Acknowledgements

The following poems have appeared previously in these magazines, sometimes in a slightly different form:

Apofenie: "The Silent One," "Shoe," "Looking Through"

B O D Y: "A Room for the Night," "Titan," "Face," "Everything Indicates," "Early Spring," "Place," "The Door," "Theft," "Night"

Circumference: "Last Century," "Two"

The Continental Literary Magazine: "The Cat"

Modern Poetry in Translation: "Call Jaroslav," "Cross Out," "I Am Growing Old," "Entrance," "The World for a Moment"

Thanks to Host Publishing in the Czech Republic for permission to publish these translations, and to Jan Zikmund of the Czech Literary Centre in Prague for his help in making this publication happen.

Jonathan Bolton is Professor of Slavic Languages and Literatures at Harvard University, where he teaches Czech and Central European literature, history, and culture. He is the author of *Worlds of Dissent: Charter 77, The Plastic People of the Universe,* and *Czech Culture under Communism,* and he edited and translated *In the Puppet Gardens: Selected Poems, 1963-2005,* a book-length collection by Czech poet Ivan Wernisch. His translations of Czech poetry and fiction have appeared in *Modern Poetry in Translation, B O D Y, Apofenie, Circumference, Best European Fiction 2018,* and elsewhere. He has been translating the work of Petr Hruška for almost twenty years, and selected the poems for this edition in consultation with the poet.

Petr Hruška (b. 1964) is a poet and literary historian who lives in Ostrava. With its environmental devastation and myriad social problems, this industrial city, located above enormous reserves of black coal, has played a major role in Hruška's poetics. His poetry has won a number of state and international awards, including the Czech State Award for Literature in recognition of his collection *Darmata* (*To No Travail*, 2012), and the Magnesia Litera, the most prestigious annual literary award in the Czech Republic, for his newest collection, *Spatřil jsem svou tvář* (*I Caught Sight of My Face*, 2022), an extended meditation on Magellan's voyage around the world. He writes screenplays, publishes a literary magazine, co-organizes literary events and festivals, and participates in civic initiatives for environmental causes and the preservation of cultural monuments in his region. Hruška also writes short stories, columns, and essays, many of which are collected in *V závalu* (*Cave-In, 2020*). He works at the Czech Academy of Sciences in Prague, specializing in poetry from the twentieth century to the present, and is the author of scholarly articles and books on Czech poetry.

In his restrained lyrics, Hruška captures moments of anger and conflict as well as love and revelation. He has said that poetry lets us perceive a world that doesn't belong to us; in this experience of transcendence, his poems find both frustration and wonder. He often asks readers to focus on sensory details even as he lets us fill in the larger emotional context ourselves. The co-ordinates of a Hruška poem are the intensity of suppressed or inarticulate emotion, the sense of limited information in a scene coalescing before our eyes, and the uncertainty that arises among friends and family when rivalry, conflict, and frustration become entangled with intimacy and love.

Collections of Hruška's poetry have been published in French, German, Polish, Italian, Hungarian, Romanian, and Croatian translation.